MORE
POETRY
COMICS

DAVE MORICE

a cappella books

The author gratefully acknowledges permission to reprint the following:

"The Red Wheelbarrow" by William Carlos Williams from *The Collected Earlier Poems of William Carlos Williams,* © 1938 by New Directions Publishing Corporation. Reprinted with permission.

"Berrigan," the cartoon, from *Nice to See You: Homage to Ted Berrigan,* © 1991 by Coffee House Press. Reprinted with permission.

"Banana" by Joyce Holland from *The Final E,* © 1978 by X Press. Reprinted with permission.

"The Liberties" by Susan Howe from *The Europe of Trusts,* © 1990 by Susan Howe, published by Sun and Moon Press. Reprinted with permission of Sun and Moon Press.

"Nothing in That Drawer" by Ron Padgett from *Great Balls of Fire.* Reprinted with permission of Coffee House Press.

"Remembered Poem" by Ted Berrigan first appeared in the magazine *Gum.*

The cartoons on pages 155, 158, 159, 164, 165, and 166 (excluding Ron Padgett's "Nothing in That Drawer") originally appeared in the magazine *Poetry Comics.*

Thanks to the following publications, in which some of the cartoons have appeared. Magazines and newspapers: *Boston Globe, City Limits, City Pages, Daily Iowan, Des Moines Register, Iowa City Press-Citizen, New York Times Book Review, Newsection, Northwest Passage, Sydney Morning Herald, 34th Street Magazine, Tractor, USA Today, Village Voice, Wallpaper Journal.* Books: *Quicksand Through the Hourglass, GED Preparation for the High School Equivalency Examination: Literature and the Arts, The Teachers and Writers Guide to Walt Whitman*

Published by a cappella books
an imprint of Chicago Review Press, Incorporated
814 North Franklin Street
Chicago, Illinois 60610

Printed in the United States of America

ISBN 1-55652-220-7

5 4 3 2 1

This book is dedicated to the first million people who read it.

Acknowledgments

I am especially grateful to editor Richard Carlin for asking me out of the clear blue to assemble a new collection of poetry comics and for making extensive comments and suggestions on the work in progress. He made the book possible!

Thanks to Fran Lee for airbrushing the colorful color on the cover.

Thanks to Michele and Samantha Soll for the lip prints in "The Siren's Song"; and to Michele for reading the manuscript and making suggestions on the cartoons. Thanks also to Milagros Quijada for her comments and help.

CONTENTS

The poems appear in their entirety unless noted otherwise. Asterisks following the titles indicate the exceptions, as follows:

    *   = lines excerpted from a larger work

    ** = words collaged together to make a new work

    *** = no words taken from the poet's work

  When the cartoon title is not the title of the source poem (or play), the original title appears in parentheses after it.

∨

THE STORY OF POETRY COMICS

IN THE BEGINNING WAS...
THE WORD!

HEY! NOT SO TIGHT, PAL!

OMNIPOTENT PENCIL CORP.

20 BILLION B.C.— THE UNIVERSE WAS JUMP-STARTED.

SOON, IN 1.7 BILLION YEARS, LIFE STIRRED ON PLANET EARTH.

I THINK THAT I SHALL NEVER TELL A POEM TO A SINGLE CELL.

Campbell's PRIMORDIAL SOUP

AMEBA POETS MADE RUDIMENTARY ATTEMPTS AT VERSE.

AS LIFE EVOLVED, SO DID POETRY.

I THINK THAT I SHALL NEVER WISH TO WRITE A POEM TO A FISH.

WELCOME TO LAND LEAVE YOUR GILLS BEHIND

WATER POETS MADE WAVES.

IN THE AGE OF DINOSAURS, TYRANNOSAURUS REX CREATED EPICS...

I SING, O MUSE, OF A PTERADACTYL. HIS HEART WAS BRAVE! HIS SKIN WAS TACTILE!

TRICERATOPS COMPOSED ELEGIES...

HALF A LEAGUE, HALF A LEAGUE, HALF A LEAGUE DOWNWARD, INTO THE TAR-PIT SANK THE SIX HUNDRED!

AND BRONTOSAURUS MADE UP LIMERICKS...

THERE ONCE WAS A BEAUTIFUL REX WHO ENJOYED PREHISTORICAL SEX IN EVERY POSITION WITHOUT INTERMISSION— AT TIMES IT GOT VERY COMPLEX!

ALAS! JURASSIC BARDS WERE DOOMED TO EXTINCTION.

2

IN THE AGE OF HUMANS, EARLY CAVE-DWELLERS RECITED POEMS AROUND THE FIRE.

ABOUT 5,000 YEARS AGO, WRITING WAS INVENTED, AND POEMS WERE SET IN STONE.

OVER THE CENTURIES, POETRY CHANGED FROM A **SPOKEN**...

... TO A **WRITTEN** FORM OF EXPRESSION.

SINCE THEN, POETRY HAS MADE MANY MINOR ADVANCES, BUT NOTHING MAJOR...

NOTHING, THAT IS, UNTIL VERY RECENTLY...

CLASSICS

TO THE READER

BY BEN JONSON

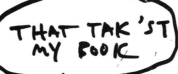

END

WESTERN WIND

BY ANONYMOUS

THE TWA CORBIES

Anonymous

As I WAS WALKING ALL ALANE,
I HEARD TWA CORBIES
MAKING A MANE ;

THE TANE UNTO T'OTHER SAY,

WHERE SALL WE GANG AND DINE TO-DAY?

IN BEHINT YON AULD FAIL DIKE,
I WOT THERE LIES
A NEW SLAIN KNIGHT;

AND NAEBODY KENS THAT HE LIES THERE,
BUT HIS HAWK, HIS HOUND, AND HIS LADY FAIR:

HIS HOUND IS
TO THE HUNTING GANE,
HIS HAWK TO FETCH
THE WILD-FOWL HAME,
HIS LADY'S TA'EN
ANOTHER MATE,

SO WE MAY MAKE
OUR DINNER
SWEET.

YE
END

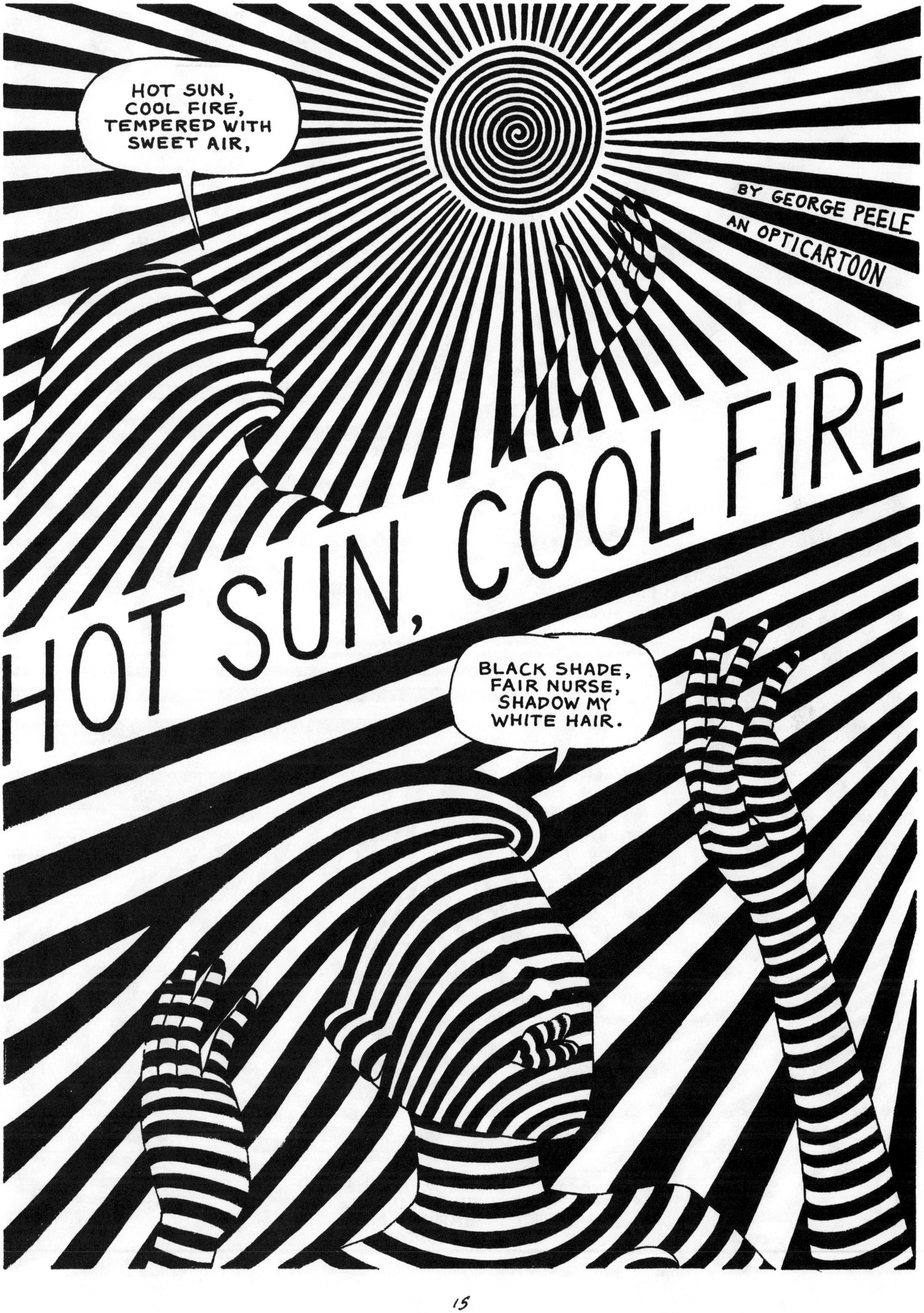

HOT SUN, COOL FIRE, TEMPERED WITH SWEET AIR,

BY GEORGE PEELE
AN OPTICARTOON

HOT SUN, COOL FIRE

BLACK SHADE, FAIR NURSE, SHADOW MY WHITE HAIR.

15

16

SHADOW, MY SWEET NURSE,

KEEP ME FROM BURNING.

MAKE NOT MY GLAD CAUSE CAUSE FOR MOURNING.

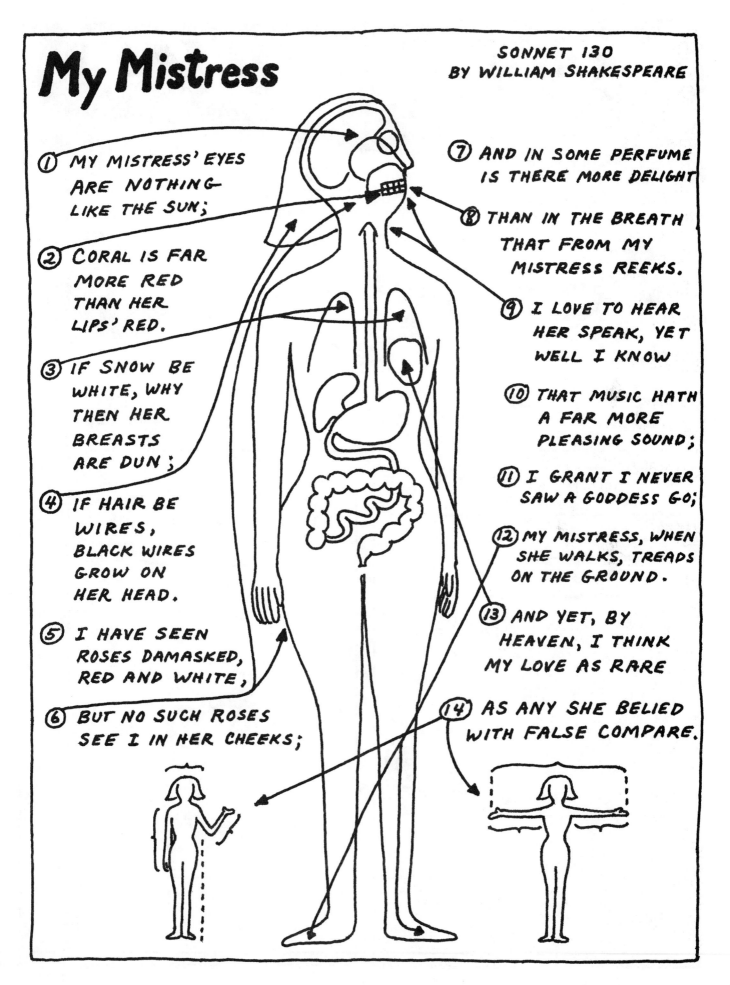

My Mistress

SONNET 130
BY WILLIAM SHAKESPEARE

① MY MISTRESS' EYES ARE NOTHING LIKE THE SUN;

② CORAL IS FAR MORE RED THAN HER LIPS' RED.

③ IF SNOW BE WHITE, WHY THEN HER BREASTS ARE DUN;

④ IF HAIR BE WIRES, BLACK WIRES GROW ON HER HEAD.

⑤ I HAVE SEEN ROSES DAMASKED, RED AND WHITE,

⑥ BUT NO SUCH ROSES SEE I IN HER CHEEKS;

⑦ AND IN SOME PERFUME IS THERE MORE DELIGHT

⑧ THAN IN THE BREATH THAT FROM MY MISTRESS REEKS.

⑨ I LOVE TO HEAR HER SPEAK, YET WELL I KNOW

⑩ THAT MUSIC HATH A FAR MORE PLEASING SOUND;

⑪ I GRANT I NEVER SAW A GODDESS GO;

⑫ MY MISTRESS, WHEN SHE WALKS, TREADS ON THE GROUND.

⑬ AND YET, BY HEAVEN, I THINK MY LOVE AS RARE

⑭ AS ANY SHE BELIED WITH FALSE COMPARE.

OUR REVELS NOW ARE ENDED.

THESE, OUR ACTORS, AS I FORETOLD YOU, WERE ALL SPIRITS AND ARE MELTED INTO AIR,

INTO THIN AIR:

BY WILLIAM SHAKESPEARE

AND LIKE THE BASELESS FABRIC OF THIS VISION,

THE CLOUD-CAPPED TOWERS,

THE GORGEOUS PALACES,

THE SOLEMN TEMPLES,

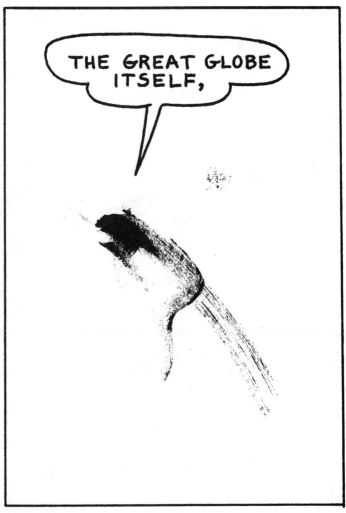

THE GREAT GLOBE ITSELF,

21

ARIEL'S SONG

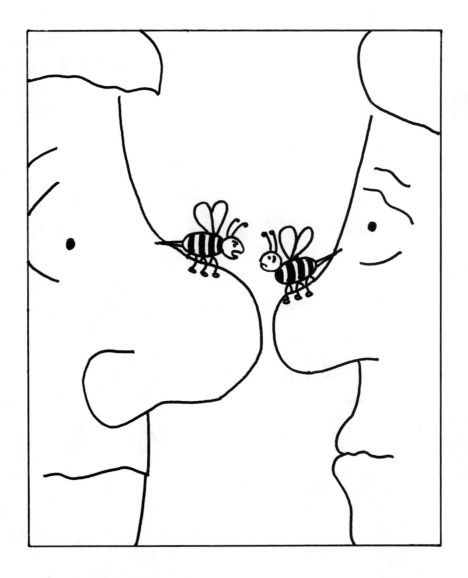

"WHERE THE BEE SUCKS, THERE SUCK I."

— WILLIAM SHAKESPEARE

To be, or not to be:

That is the question

WILLIAM SHAKESPEARE

DECEMBER 1994

SUN	MON	TUE	WED	THU	FRI	SAT
				1 TOMORROW,	2 AND TOMORROW,	3 AND TOMORROW,
4 CREEPS IN THIS	5 PETTY PACE	6 FROM DAY	7 TO DAY,	8 TO THE LAST SYLLABLE	9 OF RECORDED TIME;	10 AND ALL OUR
11 YESTERDAYS	12 HAVE LIGHTED FOOLS	13 THE WAY TO DUSTY DEATH.	14 OUT, OUT, BRIEF CANDLE!	15 LIFE'S BUT	16 A WALKING SHADOW,	17 A POOR PLAYER
18 THAT STRUTS AND FRETS	19 HIS HOUR	20 UPON THE STAGE,	21 AND THEN IS HEARD	22 NO MORE;	23 IT IS	24 A TALE
25 TOLD BY	26 AN IDIOT,	27 FULL OF	28 SOUND	29 AND FURY,	30 SIGNIFYING	31 NOTHING.

8th Day of Chanukah

Wilmer begins

Christmas

BY WILLIAM SHAKESPEARE

Thanks to the ISB&T for the use of this page.

Happy Holidays!

ISB&T

28

BUT STILL MOVES DELIGHT,
LIKE CLEAR SPRINGS RENEWED BY FLOWING,

EVER PERFECT,

EVER IN THEM-
SELVES ETERNAL.

END

END

INEXORABLE

"MY THOUGHTS HOLD MORTAL STRIFE;
I DO DETEST MY LIFE,"

—WILLIAM DRUMMOND OF HAWTHORNDEN

THE SIREN'S SONG

BY
WILLIAM BROWNE
OF TAVISTOCK

STEER, HITHER STEER
YOUR WINGÈD PINES,
ALL BEATEN MARINERS!

HERE LIE LOVE'S UNDISCOVERED MINES,

A PREY TO PASSENGERS;

PERFUMES FAR SWEETER THAN THE BEST

WHICH MAKE THE PHOENIX' URN AND NEST.

FEAR NOT YOUR SHIPS,

NOR ANY TO OPPOSE YOU

SAVE OUR LIPS ;

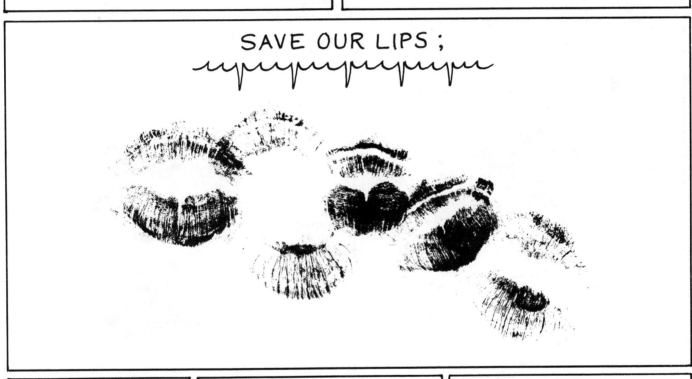

BUT COME

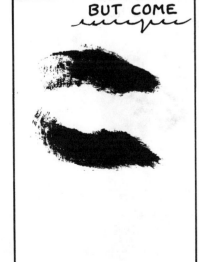

ON SHORE,

WHERE NO JOY DIES TILL
LOVE HATH GOTTEN MORE.

FOR SWELLING WAVES
OUR PANTING BREASTS,

WHERE

NEVER

STORMS

ARISE,

EXCHANGE,
AND BE
AWHILE
OUR
GUESTS:

FOR STARS GAZE ON OUR EYES.

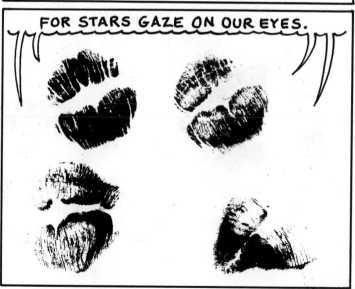

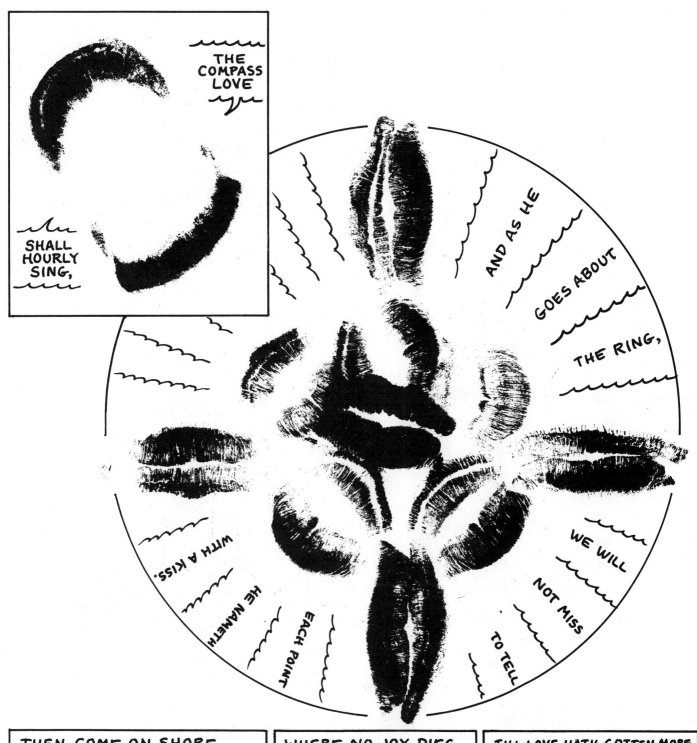

THE COMPASS LOVE

SHALL HOURLY SING,

AND AS HE GOES ABOUT THE RING,

WE WILL NOT MISS TO TELL

EACH POINT HE NAMETH WITH A KISS.

THEN COME ON SHORE,

WHERE NO JOY DIES

TILL LOVE HATH GOTTEN MORE.

END

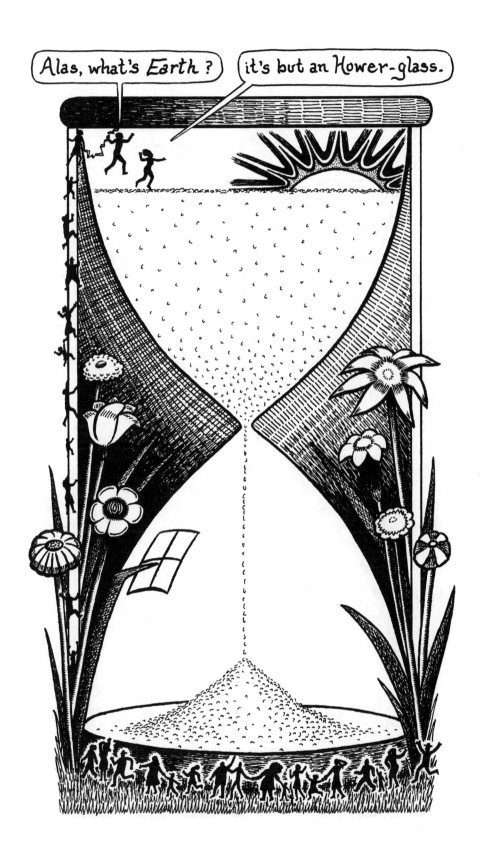

UPON PRUE, HIS MAID
BY ROBERT HERRICK

EPILOG:

40

SIC VITA

BY HENRY KING

BUDDY HOLLY

LIKE TO

THE FALLING

OF A STAR,

43

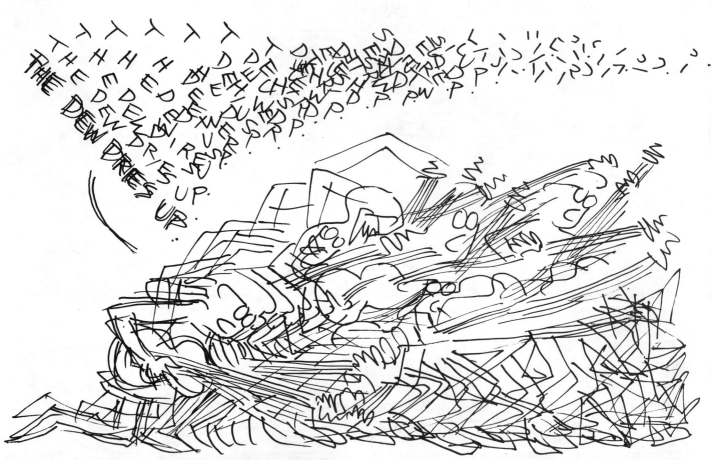

THE DEW DRIES UP.
THE DEW DRIES UP.

THE STAR IS SHOT;

THE FLIGHT IS PAST :

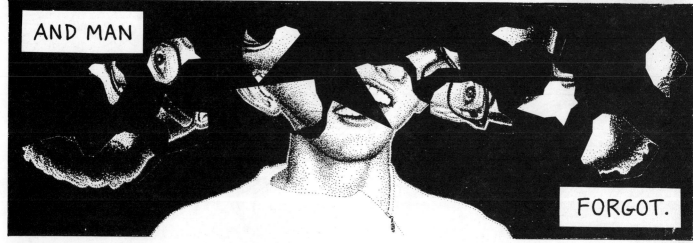

AND MAN

FORGOT.

END

To My Dear and Loving Husband

BY ANNE BRADSTREET

47

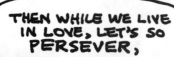

ALL HUMAN THINGS

BY JOHN DRYDEN

ALL HUMAN THINGS ARE

SUBJECT TO DECAY, AND WHEN FATE

SUMMONS, MONARCHS MUST OBEY.

END

Pious Selinda

by William Congreve

Pious Selinda goes to prayers,

If I but ask the favour;

And yet the tender fool's in tears,

When she believes I'll leave her.

52

Would I were free from this restraint,

Or else had hopes to win her;

Would that she make of me a saint,

Or I of her a sinner.

end

END

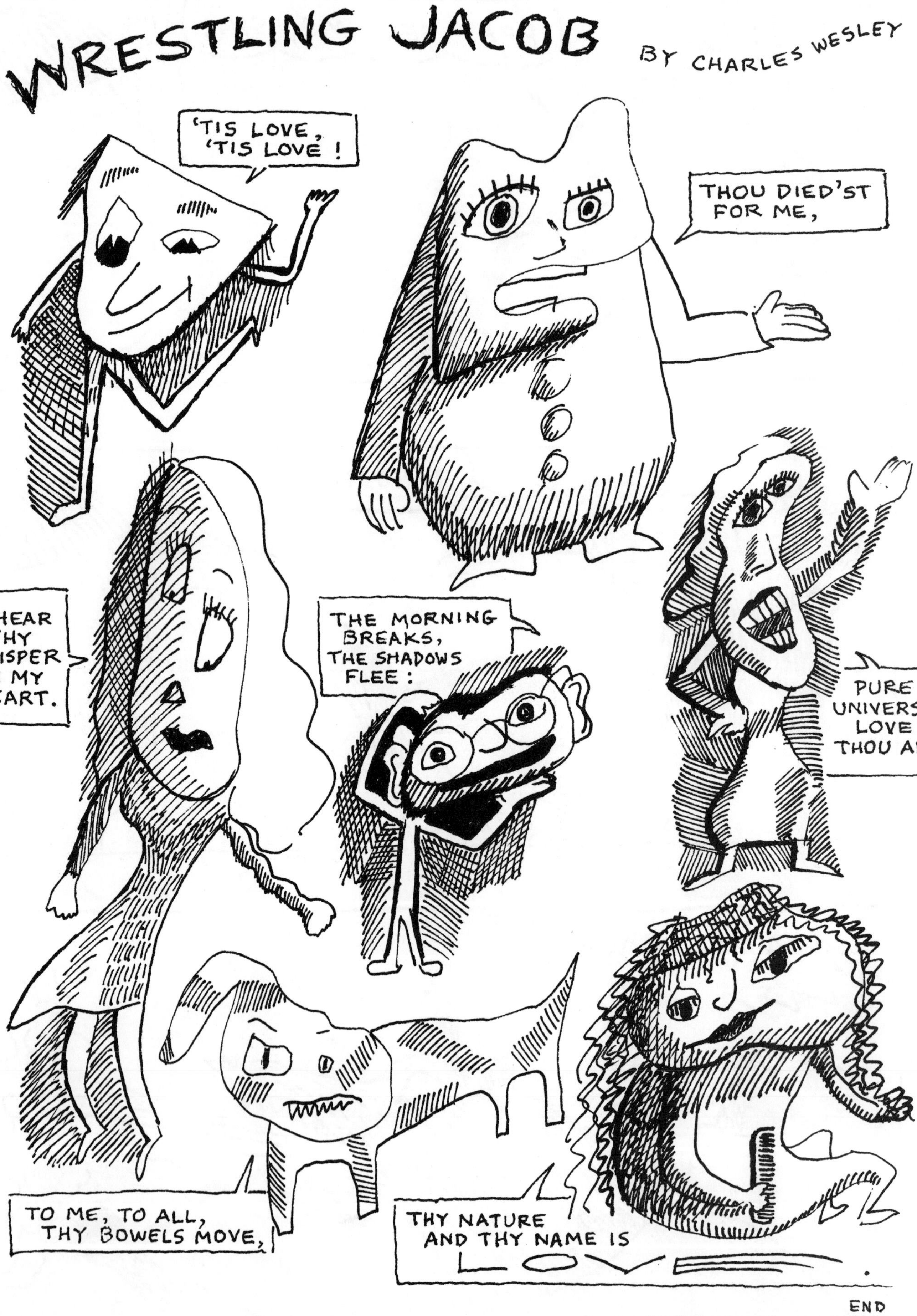

WRESTLING JACOB BY CHARLES WESLEY

'TIS LOVE, 'TIS LOVE!

THOU DIED'ST FOR ME,

I HEAR THY WHISPER IN MY HEART.

THE MORNING BREAKS, THE SHADOWS FLEE:

PURE UNIVERSAL LOVE THOU ART,

TO ME, TO ALL, THY BOWELS MOVE,

THY NATURE AND THY NAME IS LOVE.

END

SONG

"WHEN LOVELY WOMAN STOOPS TO FOLLY,
AND FINDS TOO LATE THAT MEN BETRAY,
WHAT CHARM CAN SOOTHE HER MELANCHOLY,
WHAT ART CAN WASH HER GUILT AWAY ?"

— OLIVER GOLDSMITH

A POISON TREE

BY WILLIAM BLAKE

I WAS ANGRY
WITH MY FRIEND:
I TOLD MY WRATH,
MY WRATH DID END.

I WAS ANGRY
WITH MY FOE:
I TOLD IT NOT,
MY WRATH DID GROW.

AND I WATERED
IT IN FEARS,
NIGHT & MORNING
WITH MY TEARS;

AND I SUNNÉD
IT WITH SMILES,
AND WITH SOFT
DECEITFUL WILES.

AND IT GREW
BOTH DAY AND NIGHT,
TILL IT BORE
AN APPLE BRIGHT.

AND MY FOE
BEHELD IT SHINE,
AND HE KNEW
THAT IT WAS MINE,

AND INTO
MY GARDEN STOLE,
WHEN THE NIGHT
HAD VEILD THE POLE;

IN THE MORNING
GLAD I SEE
MY FOE OUTSTRETCHD
BENEATH THE TREE.

END

MERRY HAE I BEEN TEETHIN A HECKLE

BY ROBERT BURNS

END

LUCY

FAIR AS A STAR,
WHEN ONLY ONE
IS SHINING IN
THE SKY

WILLIAM WORDSWORTH

END

Madge Wildfire's Song

By Sir Walter Scott

Proud Maisie is in the wood, walking so early;

Sweet Robin

sits on the bush,

singing so rarely.

'Tell me, thou bonny bird, when shall I marry me?'

— 'When six braw gentlemen kirkward shall carry ye.'

'WHO MAKES THE BRIDAL BED, BIRDIE, SAY TRULY?'

—'THE GREY-HEADED SEXTON THAT DELVES THE GRAVE DULY.

'THE GLOW-WORM O'ER GRAVE AND STONE

SHALL LIGHT THEE STEADY;

THE OWL FROM THE STEEPLE SING

WELCOME,

PROUD LADY!'

END

DEATH STANDS ABOVE ME

PLUS A MYSTERY POEM IN CODE
BOTH BY WALTER SAVAGE LANDOR

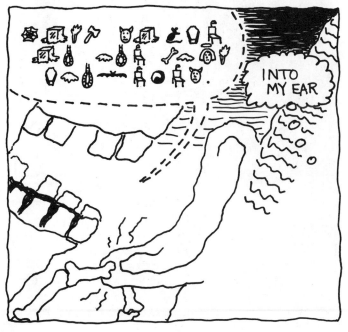

OF HIS STRANGE LANGUAGE

ALL I KNOW IS,

THERE IS NOT A WORD OF FEAR.

VISIT THE UNDERWORLD! SWIM IN THE RIVER STYX! CONVERSE WITH THE DAMNED!

ENGLISH-DEATH DEATH-ENGLISH DICTIONARY

POKE!

TWEAK!

HA! HA! HA!

YOU CAN DECIPHER THE MYSTERY POEM BY USING MY HANDY **DEATH CODE!**

A	F	K	P	U
B	G	L	Q	V
C	H	M	R	W
D	I	N	S	XYZ
E	J	O	T	

END

74

SAMUEL TAYLOR COLERIDGE

SO WE'LL GO NO MORE A-ROVING BY GEORGE GORDON, LORD BYRON

SO WE'LL GO NO MORE A-ROVING SO LATE INTO THE NIGHT,

THOUGH THE HEART BE STILL AS LOVING

AND THE MOON BE STILL AS BRIGHT.

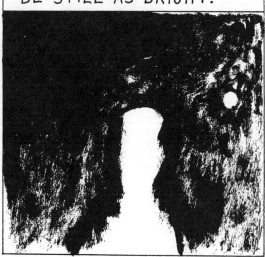

FOR THE SWORD OUTWEARS ITS SHEATH,

AND THE SOUL WEARS OUT THE BREAST,

AND THE HEART MUST PAUSE TO BREATHE, AND LOVE ITSELF HAVE REST.

THOUGH THE NIGHT WAS MADE FOR LOVING, AND THE DAY RETURNS TOO SOON,

YET WE'LL GO NO MORE A-ROVING

BY THE LIGHT OF THE MOON.

END

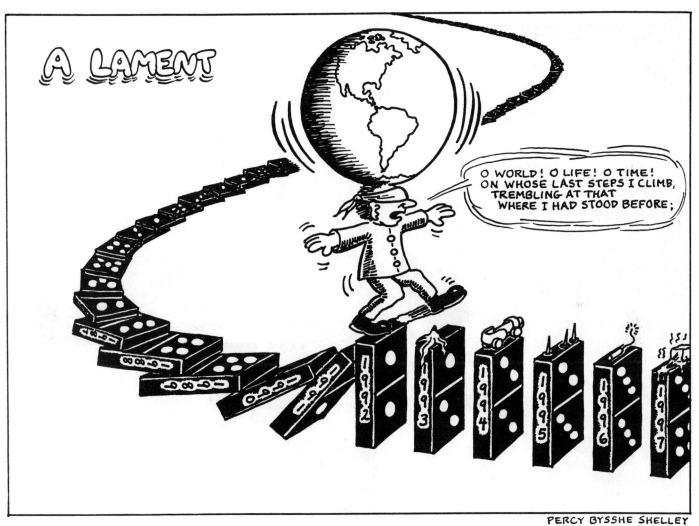

SHE FOUND ME ROOTS
OF RELISH SWEET,
AND HONEY WILD,
AND MANNA DEW,

AND SURE IN LANGUAGE STRANGE SHE SAID—
"I LOVE THEE TRUE."

SHE TOOK ME TO HER ELFIN GROT,
AND THERE SHE WEPT,
AND SIGH'D FULL SORE,

ELFIN GROT

AND THERE I SHUT
HER WILD, WILD EYES
WITH KISSES FOUR.

AND THERE SHE LULLÉD
ME TO SLEEP,
AND THERE I DREAM'D—
AH! WOE BETIDE!

THE LATEST DREAM I EVER DREAM'D
ON THE COLD HILL SIDE.

ELFIN GROT

END

83

THE TIDE RISES, THE **Tide** FALLS

BY HENRY WADSWORTH LONGFELLOW

THE TIDE RISES,

THE TIDE FALLS,

THE TWILIGHT DARKENS,

THE CURLEW CALLS;

RRRING!

THE TRAVELLER HASTENS

TOWARD THE TOWN,

TELEPHONE

AND THE TIDE RISES,

THE TIDE FALLS.

POP!

DARKNESS SETTLES ON ROOF AND WALLS,

BUT THE SEA, THE SEA IN THE DARKNESS CALLS;

RRRING!!

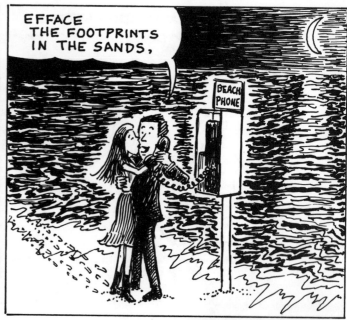

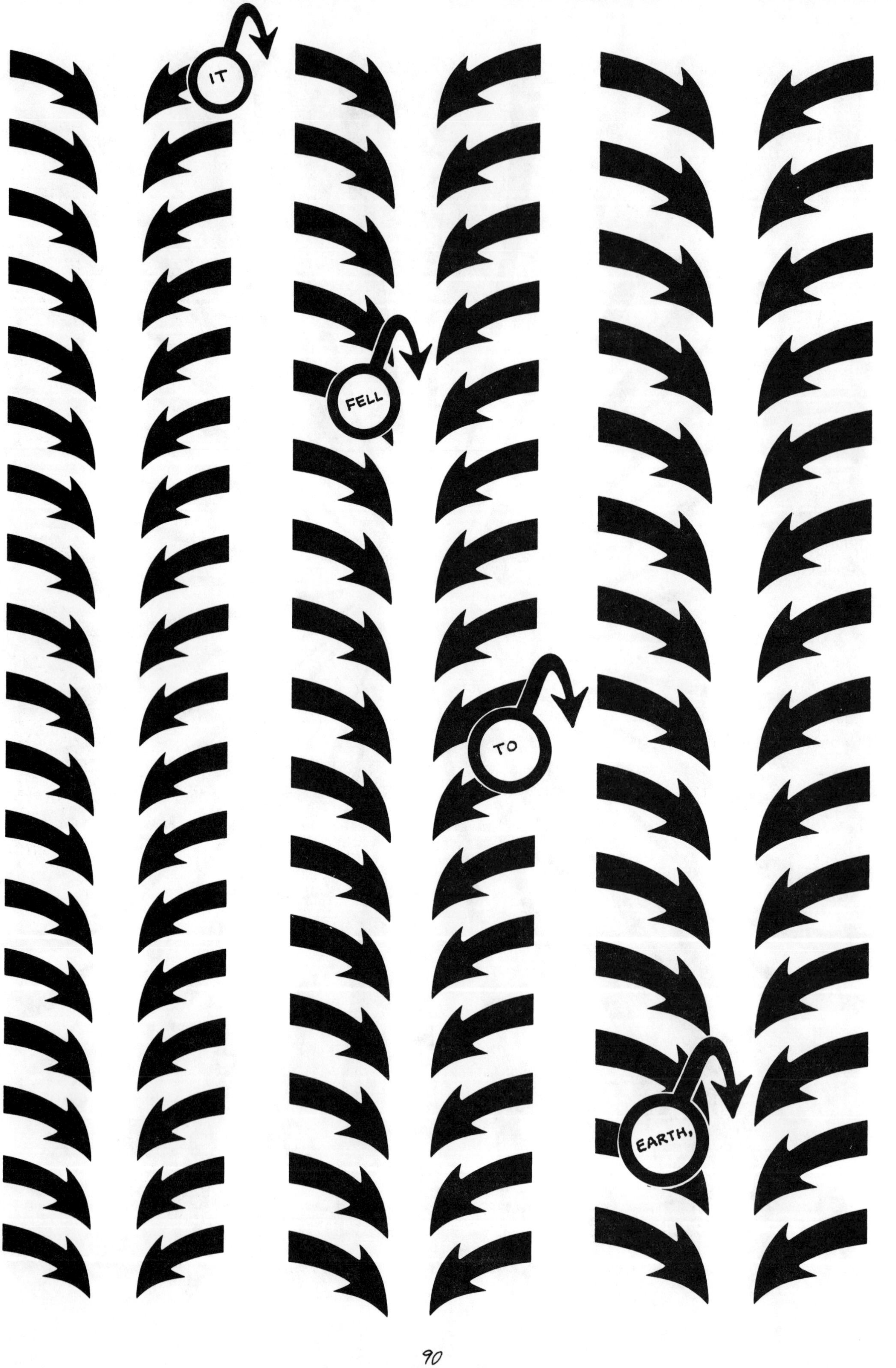
IT
FELL
TO
EARTH,

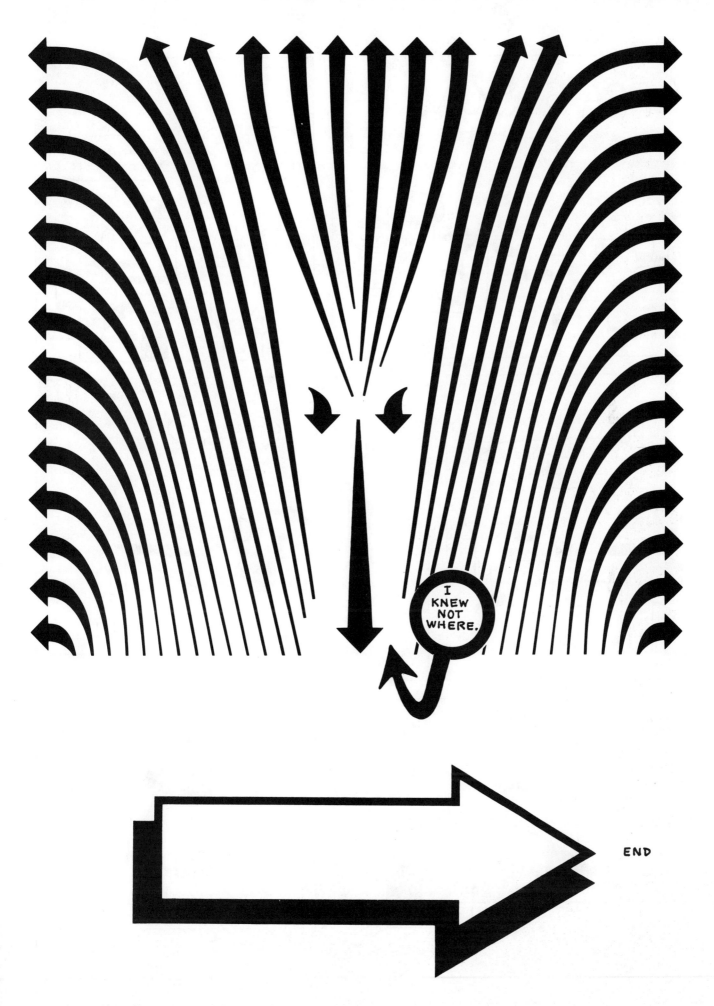

END

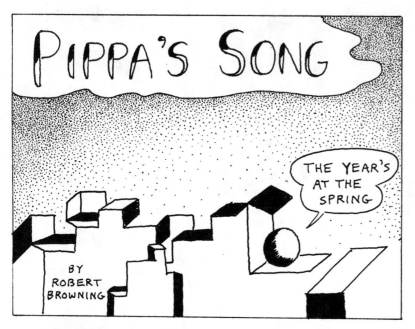

92

END

THAT'S MY LAST DUCHESS
PAINTED ON THE WALL
LOOKING AS IF SHE
WERE ALIVE. I CALL
THAT PIECE A WONDER, NOW

THE ADVENTURES OF WHITMAN

IT'S A BARD... IT'S A POET... IT'S....

— WORDS FROM "LEAVES OF GRASS" —

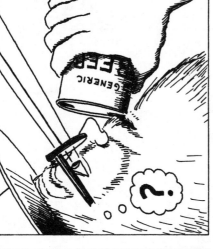

NO SENTIMENTALIST, NO STANDER ABOVE MEN AND WOMEN OR APART FROM THEM,

TURBULENT, FLESHY, SENSUAL, EATING, DRINKING AND BREEDING,

WALT WHITMAN, A KOSMOS, OF MANHATTAN, THE SON,

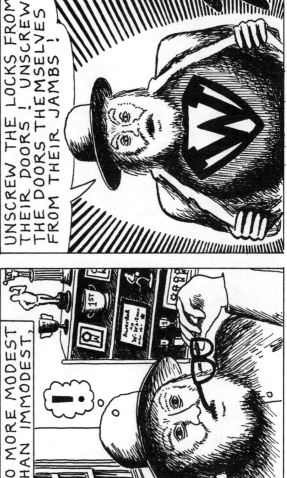

FROM PAUMANOK STARTING I FLY LIKE A BIRD,

UNSCREW THE LOCKS FROM THEIR DOORS! UNSCREW THE DOORS THEMSELVES FROM THEIR JAMBS!

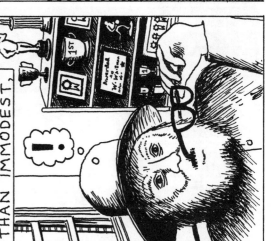

NO MORE MODEST THAN IMMODEST,

98

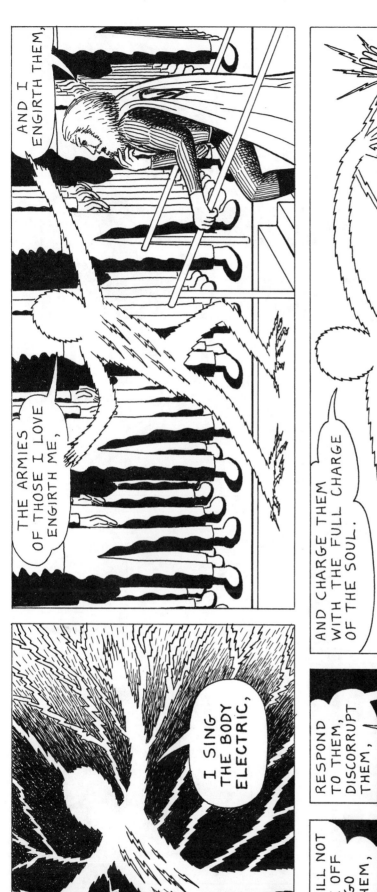

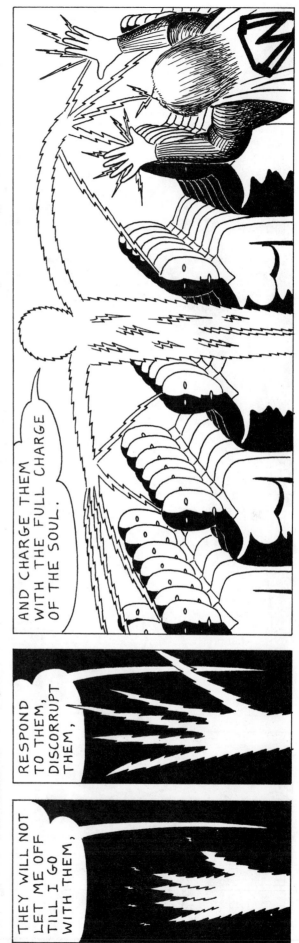

100

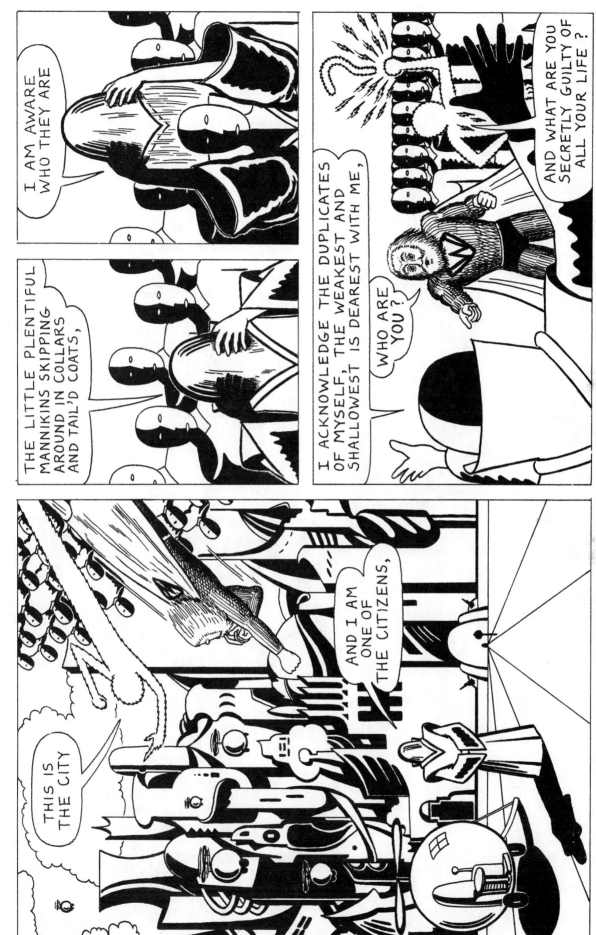

SUDDEN LIGHT

"I HAVE BEEN HERE BEFORE,
    BUT WHEN OR HOW I CANNOT TELL:
I KNOW THE GRASS BEYOND THE DOOR,
    THE SWEET KEEN SMELL,"

—DANTE GABRIEL ROSETTI

END

TITLE AND LEFT STANZA BY JAMES THOMSON
RIGHT STANZA BY THOMAS HOOD

(UNTITLED)

"SING ME A SONG OF A LAD THAT IS GONE,
SAY, COULD THAT LAD BE I?"

—ROBERT LOUIS STEVENSON

NURSERY RHYMES

119

123

127

END

to school one day,

That was against the rule;

RULE NO. 1: NO LAMBS

It made the children laugh

and play

To see a lamb at school.

END

THE OLD WOMAN
WHO LIVED
IN A SHOE

THERE WAS

AN OLD WOMAN

WHO LIVED

IN A SHOE,

134

SHE HAD SO MANY CHILDREN
SHE DIDN'T KNOW WHAT TO DO;

SHE GAVE THEM SOME BROTH

WITHOUT ANY BREAD;

AND WHIPPED THEM ALL SOUNDLY

SMACK!

AND SENT THEM TO BED.

END

LITTLE JACK HORNER

5

3534954

JONATHON HORNER. KNOWN ALIASES:
LITTLE JACK HORNER, JOHNNY THE
THUMB, JOHNNY-BE-GOOD, PIEFACE

WANTED FOR: STEALING TARTS,
DROWNING PUSSY-CATS, MURDERING
HUMPTY DUMPTY, BOMBING LONDON BRIDGE

LITTLE JACK HORNER

SAT IN A CORNER

EATING HIS CHRISTMAS PIE.

HE STUCK IN HIS THUMB

AND PULLED OUT A PLUM

AND SAID,

"WHAT A GOOD BOY AM I!"

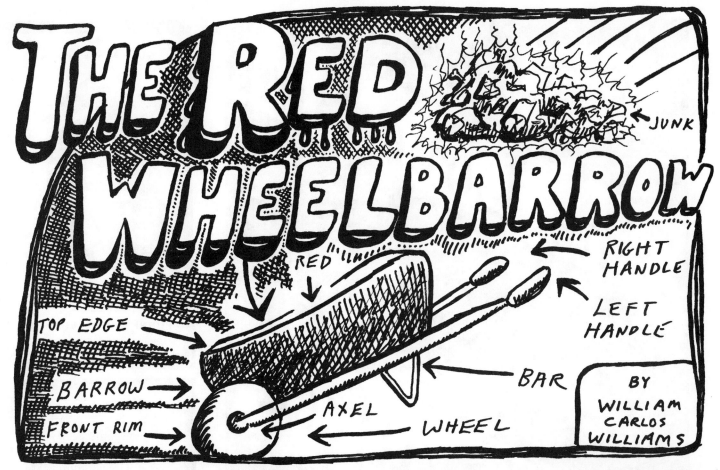

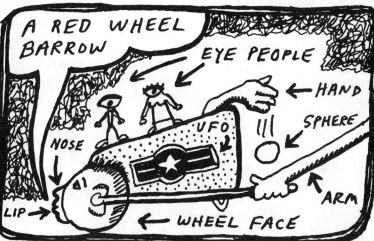

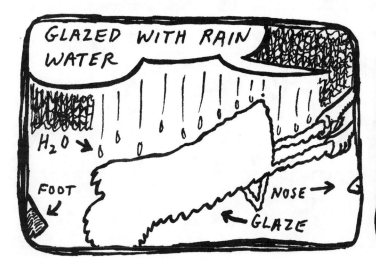

END

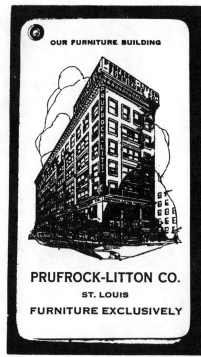

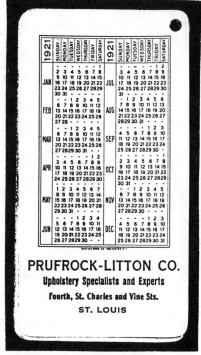

After

The Love Song of J. Alfred Prufrock

By

THOMAS STEARNS ELIOT

all the butt-ends of novels Linger here
Let us go and make a hundred revisions
half-deserted street

I have seen a sea-girl with light brown hair!
And do you dare?
ferential,
itic, cautious,
ll of high senten
imes, indeed,
t, at times, the Fool.

THAT REMINDS ME OF THE TIME I WROTE THAT LONG PIECE ABOUT A GANGSTER BY NAME OF "JR."

END

THE JUNGLE

TERENCE WINCH

A BOOK OF SPELLS

GERALD BURNS

MUSIC

BOB HEMAN

CUPOLA AT DAWN

JOSEPHINE CLARE

END

UNTITLED

BY JOHN SJOBERG

NOTHING IN THAT DRAWER

BY RON PADGETT

UNTITLED

BY MAUREEN OWEN

PEAKING

BY MICHAEL LALLY

I AM NOT A WOMAN

BY ANNE WALDMAN

THE ESKIMOS CAME LAST

BY DAVID HILTON

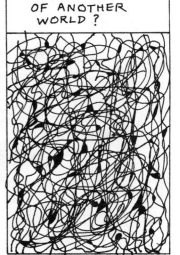

THE DISTANCE

BY DAVID CLEWELL

STARS HEATING UP THE SKY.

THINKING AHEAD THEY BURN SMALL HOLES, LEAVING THEMSELVES A WAY OUT.

I WONDER HOW TO RAISE MY VOICE FROM SO FAR, SPINNING HUNDREDS OF MILES AWAY.

ANOTHER PLANET THEY CAN'T IMAGINE LIFE ON.

HERE THERE ARE PEOPLE IN THE STREET WITH NAMES I JUST DON'T KNOW.

EVERY LETTER CLOSES WITH WE'LL KEEP A LIGHT ON FOR YOU.

END

166